Ferdinand Magellan

Struan Reid

JNF 923 MAGELLAN

Heinemann Library
Chicago, Illinois

Designed by AMR
Illustrated by Art Construction
Originated by Ambassador Litho Ltd.
Printed in Hong Kong by Wing King Tong

05 04 03 02 01
10 9 8 7 6 5 4 3 2 1

Library of Congress Cataloging-in-Publication Data
Reid, Struan.
    Ferdinand Magellan / Struan Reid.
        p. cm. -- (Groundbreakers)
    Includes bibliographical references (p.) and index.
    ISBN 1-58810-045-6 (library binding)
    1. Magalhães, Fernão de, d. 1521--Journeys--Juvenile literature. 2.
Explorers--Portugal--Biography--Juvenile literature. 3. Voyages around the
world--Juvenile literature. [1. Magellan, Ferdinand, d. 1521. 2. Explorers. 3. Voyages
around the world.] I. Title. II. Series.

G286.M2 R45 2001
910'.92--dc21
[B]
                                                                        00-058141

Acknowledgments
The author and publishers are grateful to the following for permission to reproduce copyright
material: AKG Photo, pp. 34, 40; Ancient Art & Architecture Collection, p. 7; Bridgeman Art
Library, pp. 6, 9/Fitzwilliam, 17, 27, 41; British Library Picture Library, p. 11; Bruce Coleman
Collection, p. 26; Corbis, p. 29; Fotomas Index, pp. 4, 13, 15, 25; Hulton Getty, p. 39;
Hutchison Library, pp. 23, 32; John Freeman, p. 37; Mary Evans Picture Library, pp. 5, 10, 12, 18,
20, 22, 28, 33, 35; Michael Holford, pp. 8, 16, 19, 31; Oxford Scientific Films, p. 21; Robert
Harding, pp. 14, 38; South American Pictures, p. 30; Travel Ink/David Forman, p. 24; Victoria &
Albert Museum, p. 36.

Cover photograph reproduced with permission of Corbis.

Every effort has been made to contact copyright holders of any material reproduced in this
book. Any omissions will be rectified in subsequent printings if notice is given to the publishers.

Some words are shown in bold, **like this.** You can find out what
they mean by looking in the glossary.

Contents

All Around the World

In September 1519, about 270 men set sail from Spain in five small wooden ships. This was the beginning of what was to become one of the greatest and most important journeys in history, the first voyage around the world. In charge of this small band of sailors was a Portuguese **nobleman** named Ferdinand Magellan.

YOU CAN FOLLOW MAGELLAN'S JOURNEY ON THE MAP ON PAGES 42–43.

Ferdinand Magellan was born in 1480 and lived until 1522. He spent much of his adult life as a soldier fighting in distant lands, but he is known today as one of the greatest seamen of all time. When he set out on that epic journey, he could not know that three years would pass and only one ship would return with just eighteen men, and that he would not be among them. This journey proved beyond a doubt that the world was round, not flat as many people thought, and that the continent of America, discovered 30 years earlier by Christopher Columbus, could be **circumnavigated.**

This is an engraving of Ferdinand Magellan, the great **navigator.** *Against all odds, his skill and determination led to one of the greatest sea journeys in history.*

This is an example of a European ship of the 16th century, at the time of Magellan's epic journey. Ships were incredibly small when compared with the huge ocean-going ships of today.

With a group of small, barely manageable ships and a handful of men, Magellan's journey covered 25,000 miles (40,200 kilometers) of completely unknown seas. Many of his crew fell sick and died along the way, while others mutinied and plotted to kill him. It was Magellan's strength of character and determination that drove them on to reach their destination. It was these qualities, combined with a brilliant spark of imagination and his skilled seamanship, that led to one of the greatest journeys of exploration of all time.

FACING AN UNKNOWN WORLD

Today, it is difficult for us to understand the enormous problems faced by explorers of the 16th century. It is easy for us to travel quickly from one side of the world to the other, and the world has been mapped in such detail. At that time, people believed that the world was much smaller than it really is, and Europeans had never even dreamed of the existence of the Pacific Ocean or entire continents such as Australia. When they set out on a new journey, whether overland or by sea, explorers were literally launching themselves into an unknown world. They might encounter all sorts of surprises, terrifying as well as beautiful.

Magellan's Early Life

Ferdinand Magellan was born in early 1480, the son of a minor **nobleman** named Don Roy de Magalhas and his wife, Dona Alda. He had a happy childhood, living in a large, rambling **manor house** in the beautiful northern Portuguese region of Minho. He was a very adventurous boy and early on showed great determination and courage. When he was seven years old, his parents sent him away to school at a nearby **monastery.** He was a bright boy and did well in his classes.

JOÃO II

King John of Portugal reigned from 1481 through 1495. He continued the Portuguese expeditions of exploration, started by his great-uncle Prince Henry the **Navigator.**

At the age of twelve, Ferdinand was chosen to become a **page** at the court of Queen Leonora, wife of King John of Portugal, in the capital city of Lisbon. He enjoyed his time at the court, but he also made a life-long enemy. The king's brother-in-law, Duke Manuel, was in charge of the royal pages, and for some unknown reason he developed an intense dislike of Ferdinand. This was to have a profound effect on Magellan's life.

EXPLORATION SKILLS

As a royal page, Ferdinand studied music and dancing, **jousting,** hunting, and swordsmanship. He also studied **cartography, astronomy,** and **navigation.** This had long been the practice for pages and shows the importance attached by the Portuguese to the skills needed for exploration.

A setback

King John had continued the tradition of Portuguese exploration, and it was during his reign that Bartolemeu Diaz sailed around the tip of southern Africa. Young Ferdinand was eager to join an expedition in the service of the king. But at the age of fifteen he suffered the first of many setbacks that were to affect his life. In 1495, King John was **assassinated** and Ferdinand's enemy, Duke Manuel, became king.

Ferdinand now found that every request to join an expedition was blocked. In 1504, however, at the age of 25, he did manage to join a military expedition to India. Over the next eight years he was away fighting and visited the west coast of Africa, as well as India, Malaya, the Philippines, and the fabled Spice Islands (the Maluku Islands of present-day Indonesia).

Ferdinand did well and was soon promoted. In 1512, he went to fight in Morocco, where he was badly wounded in his leg. This left him with a limp for the rest of his life that earned him the nickname "Clubfoot." Magellan was also accused of stealing some of the war **booty** captured in Morocco. Even though he was eventually cleared of this charge, King Manuel turned against him even more and refused to have anything to do with him.

This is a portrait of the Portuguese explorer Bartolemeu Diaz (1450–1500) as a young man. He was one of the explorers who opened the sea route to the East for the Europeans.

Powerful Contacts and Marriage

Magellan was now shunned as an outcast. Throughout the summer of 1516, he tried without success to secure the command of a ship bound for the East. In a last desperate attempt, he approached King Manuel directly. Now he had to endure the greatest humiliation of all as the king publicly ridiculed him. When Magellan finally asked the king for permission to find work elsewhere, the king is supposed to have replied that he could find work wherever he liked, as it was of no interest to him.

As this 16th-century map of the world indicates, when Magellan set sail, much of the world was still unknown to Europeans.

A new master

With his ears stinging from this public insult, Magellan decided to leave Portugal. He had to find backing for his plan to sail westward to the Philippines. Perhaps the king of Portugal's rival, Spain, would show more interest. And so it was that in October 1517, Magellan gave up his Portuguese nationality, left for Spain, and never returned to his homeland. He was intensely proud of his country, and this decision must have been incredibly hard to make. From that time on, the Portuguese regarded Magellan as a traitor.

A week later, Magellan arrived in Seville in southern Spain. Before leaving Portugal, he had written to a rich Portuguese **merchant** working in Spain named Diogo Barbosa, who met Magellan on his arrival. This new contact proved extremely useful to Magellan, as he now had access to influential members of Spanish society. Three men in particular took an interest in his ideas—a bishop, a merchant, and a banker. Magellan's plan was to explore the Philippines, but these three were only interested in finding a safe, direct route to the riches of the Spice Islands. These conflicting ideas would present Magellan with great problems.

Beatriz Barbosa

Magellan also met Barbosa's daughter, Beatriz, who became his wife at the end of 1517. It is possible that he viewed marriage to Beatriz as a means of securing the **patronage** he had failed to find in Portugal. However, their marriage was a great success. Beatriz was considerably younger than her husband—she was in her 20s while he was nearly 40 years old—but they were very fond of each other. In the two years before Magellan left on his expedition, they had two children.

Through his new influential friends, Magellan was eventually introduced to the young king of Spain, Charles I. It was vital for him to win the king's support, as no expedition could sail without his approval. At first Charles was suspicious, but he was soon won over. At last Magellan was given royal patronage.

King Charles I of Spain (1500–1558) is pictured here. Without his support, Magellan would never have been able to start out on his expedition.

Dividing Up the World

In 1419, Prince Henry of Portugal (1394–1460), known as the **Navigator,** was appointed governor of the Algarve region in southern Portugal. He built a palace and a church at Sagres, near Cape St. Vincent, the most southwesterly point of Europe, and called the end of the world by Europeans. He also built an observatory (where the planets and stars could be observed), a shipyard, and a school of **navigation.** At the school, students studied the art of **cartography,** and expeditions were planned and equipped. The expedition led by Ferdinand Magellan was the crowning glory of this **Age of Exploration.**

New horizons

Gradually, over the years, more Portuguese expeditions sailed further and further down the coast of Africa. In August 1487, King John II of Portugal (who reigned from 1481 to 1495) sent out an expedition led by Bartolemeu Diaz. He had been told to open up the sea route around Africa's southern tip. The following year, in 1488, he rounded the tip of Africa and sailed into the Indian Ocean.

This is Prince Henry of Portugal. His inspiration led to the journeys that would open the world to Europeans.

INTO THE UNKNOWN

Prince Henry's aim was to find a way around Africa to the East, and in all, he sent out fourteen expeditions over twelve years. Although the area opened up by his sailors was relatively small compared to that of Magellan's, they took the first and most difficult steps into the unknown.

In 1492, Christopher Columbus, who came from the Italian city of Genoa but had Spanish backing, set off westwards across the Atlantic Ocean hoping to reach the rich lands of the East. When he finally hit land, he thought he had found the route to India. In fact, he had become the first European to reach the islands off the coast of Central America.

Intense rivalry grew up between Spain and Portugal. In order to avoid a war between them, Pope Alexander VI drew up the Treaty of Tordesillas in 1494, which divided the world in two. Under this agreement, Africa, India, the islands of present-day Indonesia, and the tip of Brazil became part of the Portuguese **empire,** while the rest of America and the Pacific were to be ruled by the king of Spain.

This portrait is of the Portuguese navigator Vasco da Gama (1460–1524). His discovery of the sea route to India led to great riches pouring into Portugal.

In 1497, Vasco da Gama set sail from Portugal with 4 ships and 170 men. They rounded the tip of Africa and reached Calicut on the west coast of India after a total of ten months at sea. Over the following years, Portugal set up a huge trading empire in the East and became one of the richest and most powerful countries in the world.

Preparation for the Expedition

With the king of Spain's backing, Magellan was now at last able to organize his expedition. His instructions were to sail for the Spice Islands and then on to the Philippines, which he was to claim for Spain. But, despite King Charles's support, enemies were working against him.

Sabotage

Furious that Magellan was now supported by the king of Spain, King Manuel of Portugal sent spies to gather information and disrupt Magellan's preparations. They stole many of the food supplies and replaced some with moldy food. As if this was not enough, Magellan's three important financial backers tried to persuade King Charles to change the nature of the expedition from one of exploration to one of trade. They were only interested in making money.

They also planted their own men in the crew, so that three out of the five captains would be working directly for them. By the time the expedition was ready to leave, nearly a third of its members were working against Magellan.

This is an illustration of the port of San Lucar, Seville. It was one of the most important ports in Europe. Many voyages of exploration, including Magellan's, set sail from here.

Loading supplies

The ships were refitted throughout the summer and fall of 1518. By the following summer, all the crew members had been chosen. The expedition would be away for at least two years, so enormous amounts of long-lasting food—salted meat, biscuits, beans, rice, onions, wine, and water—were loaded on board.

Other supplies included rolls of canvas for the sails, blocks of timber for repairing the **hulls,** and barrels of **tar** and **tallow** for keeping them watertight. There were instruments and bundles of maps for **navigation,** and weapons for protection. Finally, the items for trading in the Spice Islands were loaded. These included copper bars, "quicksilver" (mercury) in flasks, knives, bells, brass and copper bracelets, mirrors, and brightly colored cloth.

Magellan bought five ships, called naos, for the expedition. Naos were very small compared to the ocean-going ships of today, with three masts, square sails, and simple decks that went up at the back and front. The Portuguese **consul** in Spain reported to King Manuel that the ships were "old and of no great size. And their timbers were rotten and soft as butter. Indeed, I would not care to venture to sea in them, even as far as the Canaries!" In the end, however, these five ships—the *Trinidad,* the *San Antonio,* the *Victoria,* the *Concepción,* and the *Santiago*—turned out to be very strong.

This is the present-day Spanish city of Seville. In October 1517, Magellan entered Seville for the first time. He was to leave two years later on his epic voyage.

The Journey Begins

You can follow Magellan's journey on the map on pages 42–43.

After months of preparation, Magellan and his five ships were ready to depart. On September 20, 1519, with Magellan commanding the *Trinidad,* they sailed out of the harbor of San Lucar de Barrameda near Seville and headed for the Atlantic Ocean. On that day, a record was made in the books of the trading company backing Magellan: "20 September 1519, five ships and 277 men embarked into the Sea of Mares." As night fell, a brilliant full moon lit up the sky, and the sea was perfectly calm. It was a promising start to the adventure.

ANTONIO PIGAFETTA

Traveling with the expedition was an Italian named Antonio Pigafetta. His job was to keep a record of all he saw and the different people they encountered along the way. Most of our information about the expedition comes from his diary, which was published two years after his return to Spain. As well as the wonderful sights they saw, he recorded the terrible conditions the men had to endure—the rotting food, the bitter cold, and the violent storms that tossed the ships around like toys.

These are two pages from Antonio Pigafetta's account of Magellan's journey. If Pigafetta had not kept this detailed record, Magellan's incredible achievement might have been forgotten.

A deadly message

The first few days after leaving Spain were quiet and peaceful. But, unknown to Magellan, trouble was already brewing. On September 26, the ships reached Tenerife in the Canary Islands, which Pigafetta describes as "a fairy, mist-encompassed island, with the spire of the Pica de Teide [a mountain] soaring high into the clouds as though to shipwreck the moon." As soon as they arrived, a ship from his father-in-law, Barbosa, brought Magellan the message that three of his captains were planning to kill him in Tenerife.

This image of West Africa and the Canary Islands is from the Vicomte de Santarem's Atlas of Mappaemundi and Portolans, 1556. The island of Tenerife, in the Canaries, was the first port of call for Magellan and his ships.

Magellan knew who the captains were, and he had an idea when they would strike. When he called a meeting to discuss the next stage of the journey, the three tried to provoke an argument. But Magellan kept cool and agreed to their demands. He was humiliated, but at least he was alive. One of the captains, Juan de Cartagena, wrote in his diary: "*El Patituerto* [Clubfoot] showed no spirit."

For some weeks after this incident, the three captains continued to provoke Magellan. But then Cartagena went too far by calling for a **mutiny.** This was the opportunity Magellan had been waiting for. Swiftly he had Cartagena arrested and locked up in chains. Stunned by this action, the others backed down. Magellan had shown them all who was really in command, but the atmosphere on board the ships remained very tense.

The Art of Navigation

In Magellan's time, there were very few **navigation** instruments available to sailors. For thousands of years, sailors had found their way around the seas by following coastlines and using islands as landmarks. When there was no land in sight, they used the position of the Sun, Moon, and stars and the direction of the winds and waves to guide them. But these were not very reliable guides, and ships often got lost, were smashed against rocks, or ran aground. Magellan and his crew were incredibly brave to set sail knowing so little of what lay ahead and with so few instruments to help them.

Steering, speed, and depth

Ships were steered using a rudder. This was a large wooden "wing" beneath the water at the stern (back) of the ship. It was connected to a long wooden arm called a whipstaff, which could be moved from side to side by a sailor standing on deck.

Sailing ships depended upon the wind to push them along. Their speed could be adjusted by altering the position and number of sails. But if they were sailing into the wind, ships had to zigzag their way along in an exercise called "tacking."

An engraving shows Magellan with some of the instruments of navigation used by sailors of the 16th century. He is holding a pair of dividers, used for measuring distances on maps.

Sailors used a piece of flat wood called a log to measure the ship's speed. This was attached to a length of knotted rope and thrown over the stern into the water. The faster the rope unwound, the faster the ship was traveling. The depth of the water was measured with a lead weight on a rope that was thrown overboard.

Early sailors, when close to land, could rely on the three *Ls*: Lookout, Lead-line, and Log. But once out of sight of land, the sailors needed other instruments to guide them, such as the astrolabe (to measure the position of stars and planets) and the **compass.**

Sailors could calculate their latitude—how far they were north or south of the **Equator.** They used instruments, such as the **cross-staff,** the **backstaff,** and the astrolabe, to measure the height of the midday sun or a star above the horizon. With the help of tables, which were first produced in Lisbon in 1509, they could work out the ship's latitude.

This Italian mariner's compass is from the 16th century. The compass is still used today for working out direction by sailors, and also by mountaineers and walkers. A needle of magnetized metal always points north. At a glance, sailors can then calculate south, east, west, and all the positions in between.

Stranded in the Doldrums

YOU CAN FOLLOW MAGELLAN'S JOURNEY ON THE MAP ON PAGES 42–43.

The fleet continued its way south towards the **Equator.** The weather was perfect, with clear skies, calm seas, and a fresh breeze blowing them along. But as they neared the Equator toward the end of October, they encountered the first of many violent storms. The small wooden ships were battered from side to side by huge waves, and the sky was filled with lashing rain and lightning. The terrified crew had to endure this for two whole weeks.

ST. ELMO'S FIRE

During the storms, the sailors witnessed a strange phenomenon known as St. Elmo's Fire. This is a natural effect caused by the electricity in the atmosphere. It was named after St. Elmo, the patron saint of seamen. It caused the ships' rigging (sail ropes) and masts to glow with a bright light, and was taken as a sign that the saint was protecting the ships and their crews. Pigafetta (see box, page 16) wrote in his diary: "During these tempests the body of St Elmo appeared to us several times. In particular on a night when the sky was especially dark and the storm especially violent, the saint appeared in the guise of a lighted torch at the head of the mainmast. . . ."

This illustration is based on Christopher Columbus's report of St. Elmo's fire, which he saw in 1493. The strange electrical glow can be seen at the top of the ship's masts.

At last the storms ended. According to Pigafetta, "Suddenly the fire vanished and the sea grew calm." The sailors were relieved at the change, but now they entered an area known as the **doldrums.** Everything was dead calm, the atmosphere became very heavy, and the sea looked like thick syrup.

Although the surface of the water was perfectly still, strong undercurrents pushed and pulled the ships in all directions.

They were caught in this strange area for three weeks. As the blazing sun beat down on them, the heat melted the **caulking** in the timbers, so the ships leaked, and the food on board started to rot. Many sailors fainted in the heat.

A killer disease

Things seemed to be going from bad to worse for Magellan. They had been away from Spain for just ten weeks, but even now the sailors were showing signs of **scurvy.** Seamen on long journeys often fell ill and sometimes died from this disease. Symptoms include weakness, loose teeth, and bleeding gums. It was not known until the 20th century that scurvy is caused by a lack of vitamin C. This is found in fresh fruit and vegetables, which were not taken on long journeys in Magellan's time, as their importance was not recognized and there was no way of preserving them.

It was not realized until the late 18th century that fresh fruit and vegetables can prevent the deadly disease of scurvy, which is caused by a lack of vitamin C. Until then, scurvy was one of the main causes of death among sailors.

South America

After weeks of being stranded in merciless heat under leaden skies, a small breeze caught the sails of the ships. The strong undercurrents had slowly drawn them out of the **doldrums,** and the **trade winds** now began to push the ships along. They were only just in time—if Magellan's crew had had to stay any longer in the heat, many of them might have died.

Landfall

YOU CAN FOLLOW MAGELLAN'S JOURNEY ON THE MAP ON PAGES 42–43.

By the beginning of December 1519, the ships were in full sail and heading for the coast of Brazil. But Magellan had to be very careful, as treacherous **coral reefs** lay off the Brazilian coastline, and many ships had been wrecked on them. He ordered a round-the-clock lookout to avoid possible disaster. On December 8 they sighted land, but Magellan decided to continue sailing southward, as they were entering Portuguese territory and could be in trouble if they landed. A few days later they were out of Portuguese waters. On December 13, they dropped anchor in one of the most beautiful harbors in the world, in what is now Rio de Janeiro, Brazil.

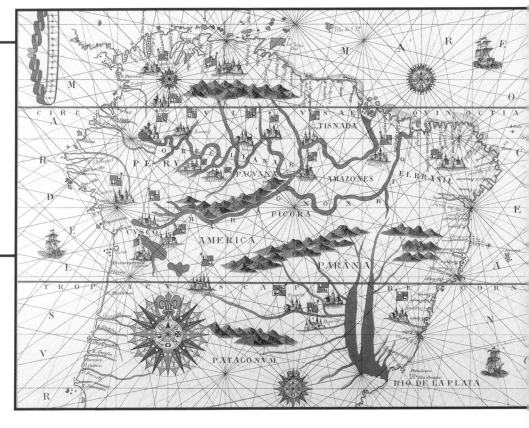

A 16th-century map of South America shows some of the places Magellan visited on his journey south in 1519–20.

The local people, the Guarani, were very friendly and welcomed the visitors. One of Magellan's crew members had been there before and could speak some of the Guarani language, so he was able to bargain for fresh food and water. The exhausted sailors went ashore and feasted on grilled fish, roasted pig, **cassava,** and sugar-cane. In exchange they gave the Guarani some of the goods they had brought from Spain, such as knives and mirrors.

The Europeans remained for two weeks in this land of paradise. Wooden barrels were cleaned out and filled with fresh water. The ships' holds were stocked with fresh vegetables and fruits such as yams, pineapples, and melons, and pork was cut up and salted to preserve it. Eventually, everything was ready for their departure and, as the ships sailed away from the coastline, a flotilla of little boats carried many of the Guarani people to wave them goodbye.

SHIP REPAIRS

When the five ships dropped anchor, there was important work to be done. They were sailed onto the beach, and their storm-damaged **hulls** were repaired. Timbers were replaced and the **caulking** patched up, so that the hulls would be watertight again. Torn sails were taken down and stitched up.

This is a view of the port of Rio de Janeiro in Brazil. Magellan and his crew found refuge here when it was an unspoiled bay.

Magellan's Hopes Are Dashed

Leaving this paradise behind them, Magellan and his crew sailed swiftly down the South American coast. For the last days of 1519 and into 1520 they made good progress, traveling at a rate of about 100 miles (160 kilometers) a day. The crew was refreshed and in good spirits, and Magellan was very optimistic.

The passage to the West

Magellan was certain they were close to discovering El Paso, "The Passage," which would lead them out of the Atlantic into the sea beyond, and so to the riches of the Spice Islands. The passage had been described to Magellan some years before by John of Lisbon, the foremost **navigator** in Portugal. Magellan also wanted to explore the large area of land that was thought to exist a short distance beyond the tip of South America. This was known as Terra Australis Incognita, the "Unknown Southern Land."

This is a view of the port of Buenos Aires in Argentina. This city is built at the mouth of the River Plate, which Magellan at first believed must be El Paso.

Bitter disappointment

On January 11, 1520, the ships rounded a headland and saw, stretching before them, a vast expanse of water. Magellan was convinced that this must be El Paso, and he sent one of his ships, the *Santiago*, to explore it. He and the other ships continued south in search of Terra Australis.

But when the ships met up again a few days later, the men had disappointing news to share. Magellan had been unable to find the Southern Land, while the stretch of water he believed must be El Paso turned out to be nothing more than the mouth of a large river (now called the River Plate).

Magellan was stunned by this news and refused to believe it at first. He led the fleet into the channel but, as the water got shallower and shallower, he accepted that the short-cut to the Spice Islands was not here.

This was not only a bitter blow to Magellan, but the disappointment undermined the morale of his captains and crew. **Mutiny** was brewing once again. The captains urged Magellan to head for the Spice Islands by a known eastward route, while the crew wanted to return to Rio de Janeiro. But he was not to be swayed. He was determined to find El Paso and, despite the grumblings of his captains and crew, in February the ships left the river and continued southward. From then on they were entering waters that had never before been sailed by Europeans.

YOU CAN FOLLOW MAGELLAN'S JOURNEY ON THE MAP ON PAGES 42–43.

This is a 16th-century map of the southern tip of South America. El Paso, which Magellan was determined to find, can clearly be seen linking the two seas on either side.

Mutiny!

For the first few days the journey went well. The crews kept the ships close to the South American coastline, searching for the opening to El Paso. But there was still no sign of the passage, and the further south they sailed, the fiercer the waves and the colder the temperature became. Sometimes the winds blew so strongly against the ships that they were blown backwards.

A grim determination

The fleet continued south for eight weeks. It became so cold that the sails and rigging became weighed down with ice. Magellan's ship, the *Trinidad,* led the others, picking its way through the unknown waters, which had razor-sharp rocks lying beneath the foaming waves. The captains complained even louder. They felt that Magellan was possessed by some kind of madness in his determination to find El Paso.

These South American seals are diving into the sea. Magellan's crew was amazed when they saw these, and many other strange-looking animals and birds, for the first time.

Towards the end of March, Magellan saw that the exhausted sailors could go no further. He ordered the ships to drop anchor in the Bay of San Julian, and the sailors were sent to gather wood to build huts on the shore. As they looked around them, they must have felt that they had arrived in the most desolate region on earth. There was no sign of any other humans. Their only companions, as Pigafetta says, were extraordinary-looking animals "the like of which no Christian man had e'er set eyes on." We know them today as penguins and seals.

During the night of April 1, captains Quesada and Cartagena led 30 sailors to capture the *San Antonio*. By the following morning, Magellan was left in control of only two ships, his own *Trinidad* and the *Santiago*. He knew he had to act quickly or all would be lost. He sent one of his loyal officers, Gonzales de Espinosa, with a letter to Captain Mendoza on the *Victoria*. As Espinosa handed the letter to the captain, he stabbed Mendoza to death. Other sailors loyal to Magellan then scrambled on board the *Victoria* and recaptured the ship. Cartagena and Quesada panicked and tried to escape, but the *San Antonio* was captured, and the *Concepción* quickly surrendered.

This 16th-century woodcut illustration gives us an idea of how officers on Spanish ships dressed in Magellan's time.

In Pigafetta's words:

"The rebels were swiftly punished. Cartagena . . . was marooned [abandoned], and Quesada was executed. The crew who had taken an active part in the insurrection [rebellion] were condemned to work in chains . . ."

The bodies of Mendoza and Quesada were strung up and left hanging for three months to remind the rest of the party that Magellan was in charge and would not be challenged again.

Magellan Discovers El Paso

Magellan had broken the **mutiny,** but he and his men still had to face the bitterly cold winter months ahead. As the huts were being built, the crew members who had mutinied were set to work cleaning the ships' **hulls.** They had to do this in their chains, sometimes waist-high in freezing water.

This is a late-19th-century impression of the five vessels of Magellan's fleet.

A nasty shock

As the food was being unloaded, Magellan was horrified to discover that half the supplies were missing. At first he thought that some of the sailors had been stealing them, but then he found out what had really happened. Back in the Spanish port of San Lucar, the Portuguese spies working for King Manuel had bribed the dockyard workers to load only half the supplies, while marking in the ships' ledgers (record books) that all had been loaded.

HUNTING FOR FOOD

They needed to make up the extra supplies, so Magellan organized his men into hunting groups to catch fish and trap animals. And what strange animals! Here is how Antonio Pigafetta described some of the then-unknown creatures: "These goslings [penguins] are black and white and have feathers over the whole body of the same size and fashion, and they do not fly, and live on fish . . . The sea wolves [seals] have a head like that of a calf and small round ears. They have large teeth and no legs, but feet attached to their body resembling a human hand."

Giants

The sailors witnessed an even stranger sight two months after their arrival at San Julian. A giant man suddenly appeared on the shore. He came from a tribe of huge people who lived nearby. "He was so tall that even the largest of us came only to midway between his waist and his shoulder. . . ." The next day, more "giants" came and were friendly at first. But when Magellan tried to capture two of them to take back to Spain, they became very angry. Magellan was forced to look for a different place to stay.

YOU CAN FOLLOW MAGELLAN'S JOURNEY ON THE MAP ON PAGES 42–43.

In mid-July, he sent out the *Santiago* under captain Juan Serrano to look further south down the coast. This ship was the smallest of the five, and in the estuary of the Santa Cruz River it was wrecked in a violent storm. The crew was rescued by Magellan.

The four remaining ships sailed to Santa Cruz, where they spent the rest of the winter. On August 23, 1520, they set sail once again in their quest for El Paso. Two months later, in the freezing waters of Antarctica, Magellan came across a wide, deep channel running directly westwards. At long last they had discovered El Paso.

These are Magellanic penguins. This species of penguin was named after Ferdinand Magellan.

Into the Pacific

Once the excitement of the discovery of El Paso had died down, some of the crew members wanted to return to Spain. But Magellan would hear none of it, and the four ships sailed into the passage. Mountains soared up on either side, and the water stretched endlessly in front of them.

The loss of the *San Antonio*

It took the ships 38 days to sail through the passage. Along the way, the crew of the *San Antonio* mutinied, and the ship slipped back towards Spain. Magellan spent three days searching for the ship, as it was carrying many vital food supplies. In the end he gave up and had to order his men to fish and hunt again to make up the supplies.

In Magellan's words:

On November 27, 1520, the three remaining ships reached the end of the passage. Magellan was certain they would soon reach the Spice Islands.

*"We are about to **stand** into an ocean where no ship has ever sailed before. May the ocean be always as calm and benevolent as it is today. In this hope I name it the Peaceful Sea [El Mar Pacifico]."*

And that is how it came to be known as the Pacific Ocean.

This is a view of the Strait of Magellan (El Paso). Magellan's journey along this stretch of water was one of the greatest events in the history of exploration.

This Spanish map of the 16th century shows ships in the region of El Paso (the Strait of Magellan) near the bottom of South America.

A vast ocean

But the peaceful sea they were now entering was in fact the largest ocean on earth. Magellan had only very simple **navigation** instruments on board—a **cross-staff, compass,** and **sandglass**—and very inaccurate maps to guide him.

After weeks at sea, the food ran out and the crew began to starve. They even ate rats, strips of leather, and the bugs and maggots in the bags of rotting food. One by one they began to fall ill with **scurvy** and die. By mid-January, more than a third of the remaining men were sick and weak.

On January 25, they landed on a small island and stocked up on fresh food and water. After a week they set sail once again. But the food quickly ran out, and Magellan knew that unless they found land within the next two days they would all be dead.

Exhausted and at death's door, the lookout was in his usual place high up on the mast of the *Trinidad*. On March 6, he was peering into the distance when he saw the hazy outline of land. Scarcely believing his eyes, he opened his mouth to call out, but he could make no sound. Bursting with excitement, he finally managed to shout: "Praise God! Land! Land! Land!"

YOU CAN FOLLOW MAGELLAN'S JOURNEY ON THE MAP ON PAGES 42–43.

The Philippines

YOU CAN FOLLOW MAGELLAN'S JOURNEY ON THE MAP ON PAGES 42—43.

It was not until the middle of the next day, March 7, that the ships were able to drop anchor. They had reached one of the islands now known as the Marianas. As they tried to disembark, they were quickly surrounded by canoes full of islanders with "light tan skin, long brown hair, and the physique of gods." The sick and weak sailors were no match for these warriors, who now began taking everything from the ships that they could lay their hands on, such as knives, mirrors, and ropes.

When Magellan demanded that they return these things, they attacked the sailors. Magellan then ordered his men to fight back, and six of the warriors were killed. The rest fled, and Magellan's ships opened fire on the villages. The crews landed and took as much food and water as they could before making a hasty departure. Magellan named this group of islands the "islands of thieves" (Islas de los Ladrones).

This is Umatac Bay and Village on the island of Guam. This was the island in the Marianas where Magellan's ships first dropped anchor on March 7, 1521.

Familiar islands

The sailors were thus able to eat their first proper food for weeks and restore some of their strength. On March 16, they sighted land once again. Magellan did not realize it at the time, but they had reached the most easterly of the Philippine Islands.

Magellan and his men spent two weeks on the island of Homonhon, which was uninhabited. There they were able to eat and rest and regain their strength. They left the island on March 27 and, the next morning, a large canoe carrying eight islanders approached the ships. One of Magellan's crew had sailed to this region before and had learned some of the local Malay language. He called out in Malay, and the islanders replied in the same language. After sailing for 550 days and enduring every sort of danger and horror at sea, Magellan now realized that they had finally reached the Philippines, which he had visited years before. He also realized that it was possible to sail completely around the world.

This illustration is from a book of 1598 entitled India Orientalis. Drawings like this were based on descriptions that Magellan and his crew gave of the flying fish and other wonders they had seen on their journey.

Tragedy and Death

The **rajah** of the local island where Magellan's ships anchored came aboard the *Trinidad*. He was called Columbu, and he and Magellan became good friends. Pigafetta describes him as "a most handsome person with black hair down to his shoulders, and two large gold rings dangling from his ears." Columbu and some of his people were converted to Christianity.

Here, Magellan and his crew disembark to the Philippine Islands. At first they received a warm welcome from the local people.

A terrible mistake

Despite their friendly welcome, Magellan's men wanted to leave the Philippines as soon as possible and head for the Spice Islands. But Magellan wanted to explore the Philippines, which had been his original plan. He also decided to set out on a mission to convert the whole population of the Philippines to Christianity. He had been told that there were some islands where the local rajahs refused to be converted, and he decided that they must be punished. A party of his men was sent out to attack the island of one of the rajahs, Cilapulapu of Mactan. Cilapulapu's soldiers were killed and his villages destroyed, but still he would not give in.

At midnight on April 26, 1521, Magellan led a group of about 60 men onto the island of Mactan. When they arrived on the shore they were met by a huge of army of about 3,000 of Cilapulapu's men. As Magellan and his small band fought their way through, he suddenly realized that they were being lured into a trap. He ordered a retreat, and most of the men scrambled back to their boats.

In the chaos, Magellan and fewer than twelve of his men were left stranded on the island. The Spaniards on board the ships refused to come to his rescue and, with no chance of escape, Magellan was stabbed to death. Four of the surviving sailors were finally rescued by the Spaniards, but Magellan's body was left behind.

In Pigafetta's words:

This was how the loyal Pigafetta described the death of Magellan:

"And so they slew our mirror, our light, our comfort and our true and only guide."

This illustration shows the moment when Ferdinand Magellan was attacked and killed by the men of the rajah Cilapulapu of Mactan.

Out of Control

Following Magellan's death, the surviving officers and crew staggered from disaster to disaster. Pigafetta wrote: "So noble a captain . . . he was more constant than anyone else in adversity. He endured hunger better than all the others, and better than any man in the world did he understand sea charts and **navigation** . . . the best proof of his genius is that he **circumnavigated** the world, none having preceded him." Without Magellan's determination and navigational skills, the officers were left floundering in these strange lands. Their first mistake was to accept an invitation to a banquet from the **Rajah** of Cebu. When the Spaniards were thoroughly drunk, the Philippinos attacked and killed most of them. Among the survivors were Gonzales de Espinosa and Juan Carvalho, who had sensed danger and managed to escape.

A band of pirates

Carvalho now became leader of the ragged crew. He decided that there were too many ships for the 115 survivors to manage, so he ordered his men to set fire to the *Concepción*. All of Magellan's books, diaries, and letters were placed on board and went up in flames with the ship. Carvalho hoped that this would obliterate all evidence of the men's treachery during the journey. As a result, for many years Magellan's name and achievements were hidden behind those of the few men who finally returned to Spain.

These are Chinese trading junks in harbor. The survivors of Magellan's expedition attacked ships like these.

With this final insult to Magellan, Carvalho ordered the *Trinidad* and the *Victoria* to set sail. Along the way, the ships attacked a Chinese trading **junk,** massacred the crew, and stole the cargo of spices. For the next four months, Carvalho and his men went on a rampage around the southwest Pacific, attacking ships and harbors. Eventually Carvalho was demoted by the rest of the crew, and Espinosa was chosen to take charge of the two ships. He restored order and discipline and, on November 8, 1521, they reached the Spice Islands.

YOU CAN FOLLOW THE ROUTE OF THE JOURNEY TO THE SPICE ISLANDS ON THE MAP ON PAGES 42–43.

Espinosa and his men spent three months on the islands. They were welcomed by the King of Tidor, who invited them to stay and trade there. Finally, in January 1522, it was time to start the long journey back to Spain. The two ships were cleaned and repaired, and their holds filled with fresh supplies of food and valuable Eastern goods. Pigafetta reported that the cargo included ". . . many **bahars** of **cloves,** plumage of the birds of the terrestrial paradise, roots of ginger dried in jars . . . very many **quintals** of pepper . . . **sandalwood,** white gold . . . robes of silk. . . ."

This illustration shows the survivors of the expedition being welcomed to the island of Ternate in the heart of the Spice Islands. The Trinidad *and the* Victoria *lie anchored offshore.*

The Journey Home

The ships were ready to leave in February 1522. But the *Trinidad* was so full of cargo that she started to leak. Espinosa was afraid that if they delayed they would miss the **monsoon** winds that would carry them swiftly away from Southeast Asia. He decided to send the *Victoria* ahead with half the men under the command of Juan Sebastián del Cano, while he stayed behind with the rest to repair the *Trinidad*. On February 13, 1522, the *Victoria* set sail westwards for Spain, two and a half years after the expedition had first left Seville.

Capture and death

As soon as the *Trinidad* was ready, Espinosa and his crew set sail east towards the Spanish territory of Panama. As they were sailing across the Pacific, however, the ship was captured by a Portuguese fleet and all the men were hanged as **pirates.**

Meanwhile, del Cano and his men had a long and exhausting journey ahead of them. Gradually, as before, the food supplies ran low and the men began to die from starvation and **scurvy.**

YOU CAN FOLLOW THE RETURN JOURNEY OF THE *VICTORIA* ON THE MAP ON PAGES 42–43.

This is a view of a beach on the Cape of Good Hope. The seas around the southern tip of Africa are some of the most dangerous in the world.

At the end of May 1522, the *Victoria* rounded the southern tip of Africa and sailed up the western coast. By July, all food and water had gone and the men were dropping dead on their feet.

Even though they were in Portuguese territory, del Cano knew he had to make a landing. So, under cover of darkness, he sailed into a remote bay on the Cape Verde Islands. Local fishermen took pity on them and gave them some rice and water, but del Cano had to make a sudden departure, leaving some of his men behind, when Portuguese soldiers arrived.

Prima ego veliuolis ambiui Curfibus Orbem
Magellane nouo te duce ducta freto.
Ambiui. meritoq̃ vocor VICTORIA: sunt mi
Vela, alæ, preciũ, gloria, pugna, mare.

VICTORIA.

Finally, on September 6, 1522, the battered *Victoria* sailed back into the harbor of San Lucar in Spain. Almost three years had passed since they had left. About 270 men had set out; only 18 returned, and their commander, Ferdinand Magellan, was not among them. The *Victoria* had sailed around the world for more than 40,000 miles (64,000 kilometers). Over half that distance was through waters never before sailed by Europeans.

In Pigafetta's words:

Among the survivors was Antonio Pigafetta, and he wrote:

"In the early morning of Saturday, 6 September we entered the bay of San Lucar, and we were only eighteen men, the most part sick . . . we went ashore, barefoot and in our shirts, to the Shrine of Our Lady of Victory, each man bearing a lighted candle."

Magellan's Legacy

Although Magellan never lived to see the completion of the expedition, the journey that he organized—and led for much of the way—was one of the greatest feats of exploration ever achieved. It proved four main points: that the continent of America can be **circumnavigated;** that the circumference (length of the curve) of the earth at the **Equator** is much greater than people had thought; that the world is round, not flat; and that travelers following the Sun from east to west gain a day. Pigafetta's accurate record-keeping proved this last point.

Nearly forgotten

For two main reasons, Magellan's achievement was played down. First, the Portuguese were furious that he had achieved so much

FERDINAND MAGELLANUS.

for their rivals, the Spaniards. They regarded him as a traitor. The Spanish crew of the *San Antonio* blackened his name to cover up their own shame and treachery. Second, although the expedition added greatly to the knowledge of the world at that time, it did not succeed in finding a quick route to the riches of the East. It brought no profit to the king of Spain, and the route was far too long and dangerous and so was hardly ever used. Today, however, Ferdinand Magellan is hailed as one of the greatest seamen that has ever lived.

This is a 17th-century engraving of Ferdinand Magellan. For many years his achievements were forgotten, but by the time this engraving was made, he was recognized as one of the greatest seamen of all time.

Those who followed

After his return to Spain, del Cano took all the credit for sailing the *Victoria* around the world. In 1525, he set out on another expedition to explore the Pacific, but was shipwrecked and died there. For the next 50 years a number of people tried to follow Magellan's route through El Paso (now called the Strait of Magellan), but they all failed.

The second great voyage of circumnavigation after Magellan's expedition was led by the Englishman, Sir Francis Drake (1540–96). He set out with a fleet of five ships in 1577. Like Magellan, Drake and his men suffered many hardships on the voyage. Storms, starvation, and sickness provoked **mutinies** among the crew. The expedition sailed through the Strait of Magellan and eventually returned to England in the autumn of 1580.

This miniature portrait of Sir Francis Drake was painted in 1581, the year after his triumphant return from the second circumnavigation of the world.

A great seaman

We might have known very little about Magellan today had it not been for the diaries of Antonio Pigafetta. Because of these, we have a record of how "Magellan's main virtues were courage and perseverance, in even the most difficult situations . . . He was a magnificent practical seaman, who understood **navigation** better than all his pilots."

Map of the Route of Magellan's Ships

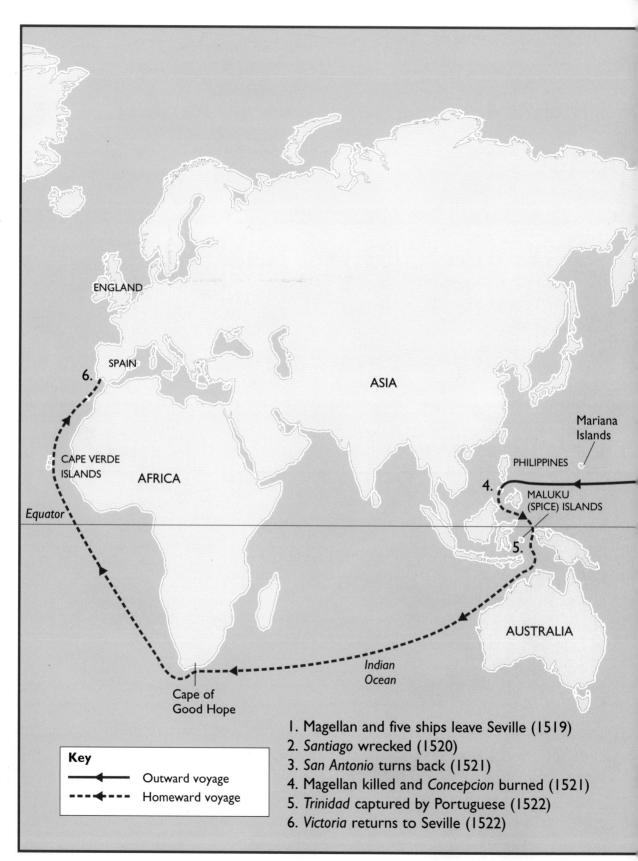

ENGLAND

SPAIN

6.

CAPE VERDE
ISLANDS

AFRICA

ASIA

Equator

Mariana
Islands

PHILIPPINES

4.

MALUKU
(SPICE) ISLANDS

5.

AUSTRALIA

Indian
Ocean

Cape of
Good Hope

1. Magellan and five ships leave Seville (1519)
2. *Santiago* wrecked (1520)
3. *San Antonio* turns back (1521)
4. Magellan killed and *Concepcion* burned (1521)
5. *Trinidad* captured by Portuguese (1522)
6. *Victoria* returns to Seville (1522)

Key

←———	Outward voyage
◄- - - -	Homeward voyage

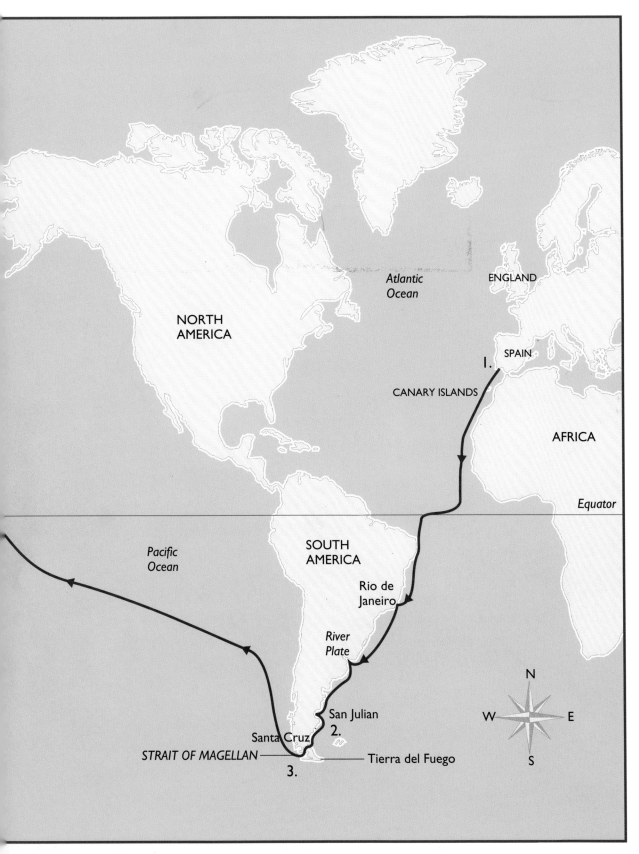

NORTH
AMERICA

Atlantic
Ocean

ENGLAND

SPAIN

1.

CANARY ISLANDS

AFRICA

Equator

Pacific
Ocean

SOUTH
AMERICA

Rio de
Janeiro

River
Plate

San Julian

2.

Santa Cruz

STRAIT OF MAGELLAN

Tierra del Fuego

3.

N
W   E
S

Timeline

1419   Prince Henry the Navigator begins his school of navigation in southern Portugal.

1480   Ferdinand Magellan is born.

1488   Bartolemeu Dias rounds the southern tip of Africa.

1492   Christopher Columbus discovers the Americas.

1494   The Treaty of Tordesillas is signed.

1495   Duke Manuel becomes king of Portugal.

1498   Vasco da Gama reaches Calicut in India.

1504   Magellan leaves Portugal for India and Southeast Asia.

1507   America is named after Amerigo Vespucci.

1511   Diego Velazquez and Hernando Cortés seize Cuba for Spain.

1512   Magellan fights in Morocco and is badly wounded in his leg.

1517   Magellan leaves Portugal forever and moves to Spain.
Magellan and Beatriz Barbosa are married.

1519   On September 20, Magellan and his fleet begin their journey around the world.
In October, Cartagena calls for mutiny, but Magellan has him arrested.

1520   April 1, Quesada and Cartagena lead a second mutiny and capture three ships, but Magellan regains control.
In October, the expedition finally discovers El Paso, now called the Strait of Magellan.

1521   Magellan reaches the Philippines.
Ferdinand Magellan dies.

1522   The *Victoria* and the *Trinidad* begin their return journey to Spain

1525   Juan Sebastián del Cano sets out on another expedition to explore the Pacific Ocean.

1577   Francis Drake begins his journey around the world.

1580   Drake returns to England, having completed the second circumnavigation of the world.

More Books to Read

Barron's Educational Editors. *Magellan and the Exploration of South America.* Hauppauge, N.Y.: Barron's Educational Series, 1998.

Gallagher, Jim. *Ferdinand Magellan and the First Voyage Around the World.* Broomall, Pa.: Chelsea House Publishers, 2000.

Ganeri, Anita. *What Would You Ask?* North Mankato, Minn.: Thameside Press, 2000.

Hurwicz, Claude. *Ferdinand Magellan.* New York: Rosen Publishing Group, 2000.

MacDonald, Fiona. Illustrated by Mark Bergin. *Magellan: A Voyage Around the World.* Danbury, Conn.: Franklin Watts, 1998.

Mattern, Joanne. *Ferdinand Magellan.* Austin, Tex.: Raintree Steck-Vaughn, 2000.

Twist, Clint. *Magellan and Da Gama.* Austin, Tex.: Raintree Steck-Vaughn, 1994.

Glossary

Age of Exploration   period from the early 15th century that lasted about 200 years, during which European explorers sailed to most parts of the globe for the first time

assassinate   murder an important political person

astronomy   study of the stars, planets, and the entire universe

backstaff   instrument used at sea for measuring the height of the Sun above the horizon, enabling sailors to calculate the latitude of their ship

bahar   measurement of weight, equivalent to approximately 400 pounds (180 kilograms)

booty   goods stolen during time of war

caravan   group of traders or other travelers journeying together with animals

cartography   map making

cassava   starchy food extracted from the root of the cassava plant

caulking   waterproof material used to stop up the cracks between the planks in a ship's hull

circumnavigate   sail or fly all the way around something

clove   dried flower bud of the evergreen clove tree, used as a spice in cooking

compass   instrument with a magnetized needle that is used to find direction

consul   official representing the interests of a ruler in a foreign country or city

coral reef   shelf beneath the surface of the sea that consists of coral that has turned into limestone

cross-staff   navigation instrument once used at sea for measuring the altitude of stars and planets, especially the Sun, which gave the latitude of the ship

doldrums   area of calm seas along the Equator

empire   large area of territories and people governed by a single ruler

Equator   line around the middle of the earth that divides the northern and southern hemispheres

hull   main body of a ship, made of wooden planks

jousting   combat between two knights mounted on horseback

junk   Chinese ship, made of wood and with very high sides, a flat bottom, and square sails

manor house in medieval Europe, a large house and the lands attached to it

merchant someone who buys and sells goods, often of one particular kind

monastery building where a religious community of monks lives

monsoon wind that blows in southern Asia, from the southwest in summer and from the northeast in winter

morale level of confidence a person or group of people have

mutiny rebellion by sailors or soldiers against their leaders

navigation skill of directing the path or course of a ship

navigator person who directs the path or course of a ship

nobleman someone who belongs to a hereditary class with special status in society

page in medieval Europe, a boy who was in training to become a knight

patronage financial support given to someone, usually by a wealthier, more powerful person

pirate someone who commits robbery at sea, usually against another ship

quintal measurement of weight, equivalent to approximately 112 pounds (51 kilograms)

rajah term used for prince or chief in some countries in Asia and the Pacific

sandalwood perfumed wood found in southern Asia, which was very expensive

sandglass time-keeping device made up of two glass bulbs, with sand trickling from one bulb to the other

scurvy disease caused by lack of vitamin C that leads to tiredness and eventually death

stand as a sailing term, to navigate in a particular direction

tallow fatty substance extracted from sheep and cattle; used in the past to make soap and candles and as a waterproofing material

tar dark, sticky substance extracted from the earth

trade winds winds that blow toward the Equator, northeast in the northern hemisphere and southeast in the southern hemisphere

Index